W9-BKQ-135

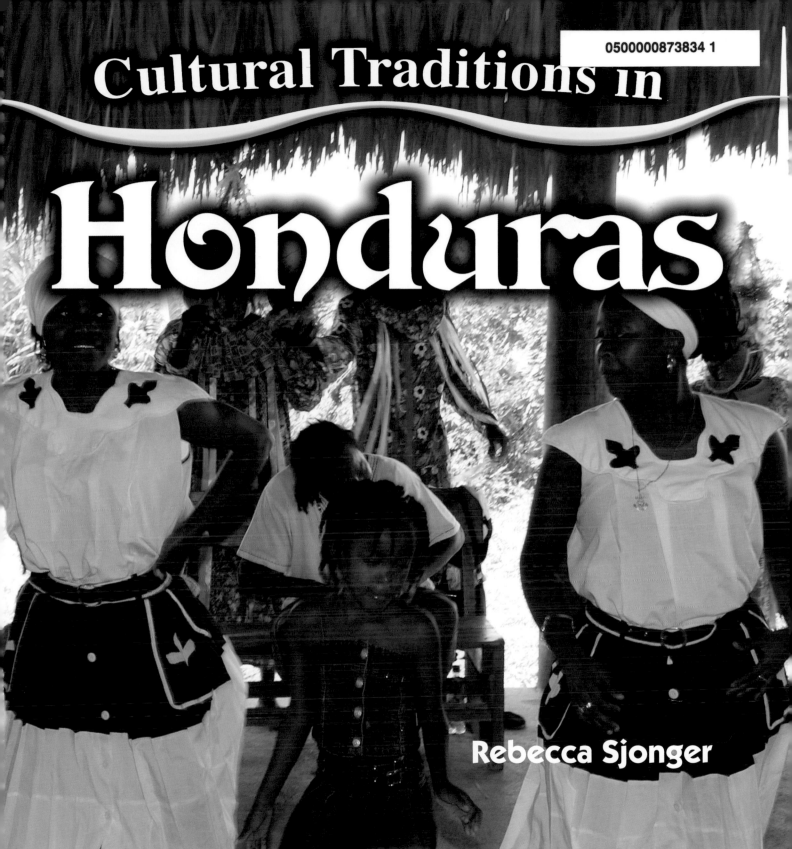

Cultural Traditions in

Honduras

Rebecca Sjonger

Crabtree Publishing Company

www.crabtreebooks.com

Crabtree Publishing Company
www.crabtreebooks.com

Author: Rebecca Sjonger

Publishing plan research and development:
Reagan Miller

Editorial director: Kathy Middleton

Editor: Ellen Rodger

Proofreader: Wendy Scavuzzo

Photo research: Abigail Smith

Designer: Abigail Smith

Production coordinator and prepress technician:
Abigail Smith

Print coordinator: Margaret Amy Salter

Cover: A coral reef in Roátan (top, background); Pulhapanzak waterfall in San Buenaventura (middle background); the brassavola orchid flower and scarlet macaw are native to Honduras (upper middle); A carved stone slab from an ancient Mayan ruin at Copan (left); A girl presents a Honduran national dish of beans, fried plantain, grilled meat and rice (bottom right).

Title page: Folk dancers in Roátan, Honduras

Photographs:
Alamy: SCPhotos, title page; Rob Crandall, p8; age fotostock, pp21, 27 (left); Dennis Cox, p29 (inset); Christian Kober 1, p31 (bkgd)
AP Images: VICTOR R. CAIVANO, p18
Getty Images: ORLANDO SIERRA/AFP, pp11, 13, 14, 15, 17, 22, 23, 25, 26, 30; Jose CABEZAS, p24
iStock: dstephens, pp 4–5 (bkgd); Nolmedrano99, p12; urf, p16;
Keystone: © Gustavo, Amador p9 (bkgd)
Shutterstock: © Diana Mary Jorgenson, front cover (girl);
© Sandra A. Dunlap, p13 (inset);
Wikimedia Commons: KES47, p11 (inset); Ramon cerritos, p19; JVC3ETA, p20 (left); ETXEVERZ, p20 (right); AlejandroLinaresGarcia, p31 (inset);

All other images by Shutterstock

Library and Archives Canada Cataloguing in Publication

Sjonger, Rebecca, author
    Cultural traditions in Honduras / Rebecca Sjonger.

(Cultural traditions in my world)
Includes index.
Issued in print and electronic formats.
ISBN 978-0-7787-8096-0 (hardcover).--
ISBN 978-0-7787-8104-2 (softcover).--
ISBN 978-1-4271-1951-3 (HTML)

    1. Holidays--Honduras--Juvenile literature. 2. Festivals--Honduras--Juvenile literature. 3. Honduras--Social life and customs--Juvenile literature. I. Title. II. Series: Cultural traditions in my world

GT4819.A2S56 2017   j394.2697283   C2017-903515-0
                                           C2017-903516-9

Library of Congress Cataloging-in-Publication Data

Names: Sjonger, Rebecca, author.
Title: Cultural traditions in Honduras / Rebecca Sjonger.
Description: New York, New York : Crabtree Publishing, 2018.
Series: Cultural traditions in my world | Includes index. | Audience: Age 5-8. | Audience: Grade K to 3.
Identifiers: LCCN 2017024405 (print) | LCCN 2017027891 (ebook) | ISBN 9781427119513 (Electronic HTML) | ISBN 9780778780960 (reinforced library binding) | ISBN 9780778781042 (pbk.)
Subjects: LCSH: Festivals--Honduras--Juvenile literature. | Honduras--Social life and customs--Juvenile literature.
Classification: LCC GT4819.A2 (ebook) | LCC GT4819.A2 S56 2018 (print) | DDC 394.2697283--dc23
LC record available at https://lccn.loc.gov/2017024405

Crabtree Publishing Company
www.crabtreebooks.com   1-800-387-7650

Printed in Canada/082017/EF20170629

Published in Canada
Crabtree Publishing
616 Welland Ave.
St. Catharines, ON
L2M 5V6

Published in the United States
Crabtree Publishing
PMB 59051
350 Fifth Avenue, 59th Floor
New York, New York 10118

Published in the United Kingdom
Crabtree Publishing
Maritime House
Basin Road North, Hove
BN41 1WR

Published in Australia
Crabtree Publishing
3 Charles Street
Coburg North
VIC 3058

Contents

Welcome To Honduras

Honduras is in **Central America**. The country's culture is a lively blend of **Indigenous**, African, and Spanish **settler** languages, religions, holidays, and festivals. Today, most Hondurans have a mix of backgrounds.

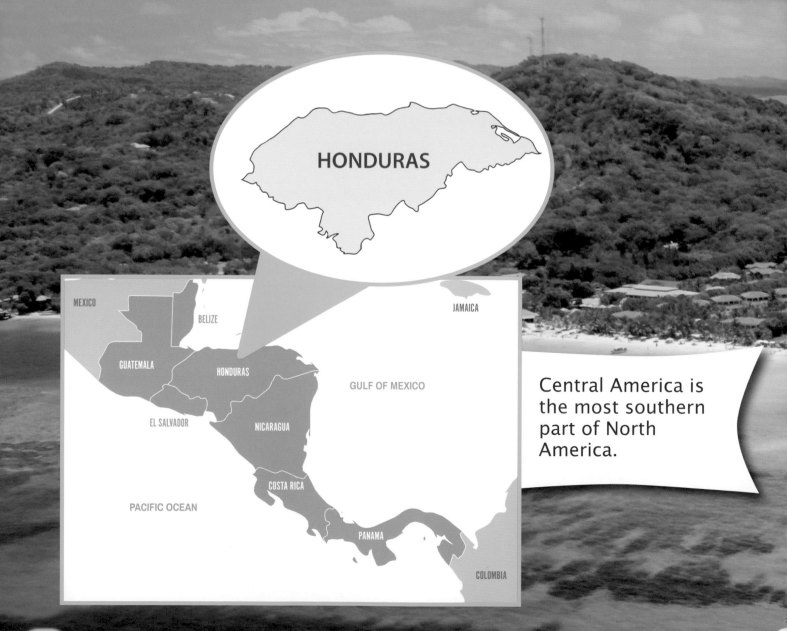

Central America is the most southern part of North America.

This book shows some of the festivals and customs that are part of Honduran cultural traditions. Most of their holidays are **Roman Catholic**. Spanish settlers brought this religion to Honduras. It is still an important part of many people's lives.

Did You Know? Several **ethnic** and Indigenous groups such as the Miskito, Garifuna, and the Pech people live in Honduras.

Fiestas are parties held for holidays and family events. Family is very important in Honduras. Grandparents, aunts, uncles, and cousins have fun together at fiestas. Even if some Hondurans do not have much money to spend on these parties, they still welcome guests with a feast.

Meals at fiestas often include tortillas stuffed with rice, cheese, or beans.

Did You Know? Honduran parents choose "compadres," or godparents, for their children. Compadres are close friends who act like parents.

Families often hold a fiesta for a child's birthday. The women in the family may fill a **piñata** with candies for the party. Instead of singing Happy Birthday, Hondurans sing Las Mañanitas.

The candy inside piñatas are often made with local sugarcane, a plant that sugar is taken from.

Happy New Year!

Like many people around the world, Hondurans have fun at New Year's. They go outdoors at midnight. Neighbors wish one another a happy New Year. Even young children stay up late into the night. On January 1, most people in Honduras wear new clothing.

Women dance during a New Year's Eve celebration in Honduras.

Some Hondurans burn dummies on New Year's Eve. They stuff newspapers and firecrackers into old clothes to form them. The dummies are lit on fire as people cheer. This custom marks the end of the old year and the start of the new one.

People may burn lookalike dummies of politicians and other unpopular leaders they feel have failed in their work.

Festival of Suyapa

Honduras shows its Catholic roots on feast days. Its villages, towns, and cities each have their own **patron saint**. Some people believe the saints help them. A calendar lists which saints to pay respect to each day. These are feast days.

The church of Suyapa is in the capital city of Honduras, Tegucigalpa.

The patron saint of Honduras is Our Lady of Suyapa. Her feast day is February 3. Hondurans celebrate it with festivals across the country that often last an entire week. They watch firework displays. Live bands play traditional music, such as salsa and reggae.

Did You Know?
Our Lady of Suyapa is a statue of the **Virgin Mary**. Many people go to see the statue during the Festival of Suyapa.

Hondurans in Tegucigalpa attend a celebration of the Festival of Suyapa.

Semana Santa

Most Hondurans celebrate Semana Santa in the early spring. It is the Spanish name for Holy Week, or the week before Easter. Semana Santa begins on Palm Sunday and includes Holy Thursday, Good Friday, and Holy Saturday. Each of these days honors part of the story of Jesus found in the Bible.

Did You Know?
Artists cover the streets with *alfombras* during Semana Santa. These are colorful sawdust and sand carpets. People shape the sawdust into Easter scenes.

The Easter bunny is not part of the holiday in Honduras. Instead, many people focus on events held by their churches. They have parades and **re-enact** Bible stories. Other people spend Semana Santa on the country's beaches. Schools and businesses close. The week ends with big family fiestas.

Thousands of people pack the streets to watch Easter parades, such as this one in the city of Comayagua.

Arrival of the Garifuna

The Garifuna are Indigenous people in Honduras. They originally lived on the Caribbean island of Saint Vincent, but were **exiled** from the island on April 12, 1797, when the British took control of it. They were sent to Roatan, an island off the coast of Honduras. Some of them later moved to the mainland.

Garifuna women perform a traditional dance. It represents the Garifuna's exile to Roatan.

These Garifuna are dancing and celebrating durring a Drum March in Tegucigalpa. It celebrates their arrival in Honduras.

Every April 12, the Garifuna remember their arrival in Honduras. They re-enact landing on Roatan. There are huge parties with music and dances in Garifuna communities across the country. Foods include fish soup and *machuca*, a paste made from boiled plantains pounded with coconut milk.

Garifuna dancers wear colorful costumes.

Pan American Day and Labor Day

Each country in the Americas is part of the **Organization of American States**. This organization works for peace and cooperation. Member countries mark Pan American Day on April 14. Honduras is one of the few places where it is a national holiday. Schools host concerts, parades, and plays.

Did You Know?
On April 14, Honduras flies the flags of each country in the Organization of American States.

Many Hondurans work in agriculture, or farming.

May 1 is Labor Day in Honduras. In some countries, it is a time to relax. In Honduras, thousands of people travel into cities such as Tegucigalpa. They march through the streets together. People carry signs asking for jobs that are safe and pay well.

Workers march in the streets wearing red and white clothing. They also carry red banners on Labor Day. Red represents the color of blood and the struggle for fair treatment for workers.

La Ceiba Carnival

La Ceiba hosts a huge carnival each May. People from all over Central America go to it. San Isidro is La Ceiba's patron saint. The week of parties centers around his May 15 feast day. One of the first events is choosing a carnival queen.

People eat, drink, and dance in the streets after the big La Ceiba parade.

Parts of the city hold carnavalitos, or little carnivals, each night. Local foods such as grilled meats are sold in street stalls. People dance to live bands playing many kinds of music. On the last day, a colorful parade, shown below, goes down the main street. It ends with a party that lasts all night long.

Did You Know?
A week before the big La Ceiba Carnival, people in neighboring towns hold their own smaller parades and carnivals.

Lempira's Day

In the 1500s, the Spanish began to settle in what is now Honduras. They did not care that people already lived there. An Indigenous leader named Lempira fought back. He led his people, the **Lenca**, in battle. The Lenca lost, but Lempira became a hero.

Did You Know?
Honduran money is called lempiras instead of dollars. A picture of Lempira is on the 1 lempira paper bill.

This statue of Lempira stands in the Honduran city of Erandique.

Hondurans hold Lempira's Day on July 20 each year. Children dress up in the traditional clothing of the Lenca people. It is made of materials such as dried corn and feathers. In some areas, they parade around their schools. Student bands march with them. In Lenca communities, children parade along main streets. Large crowds cheer them on.

Many Lenca people are skilled potters. Pottery is making items, such as the pot below, out of clay.

Children's Day and Teachers' Day

Honduran children love September 10! It is Children's Day. The elementary schools close, and students go to fun events held by community groups and businesses. There, children enjoy party games, face painting, and piñatas. The day is as exciting as a birthday for families who cannot afford big fiestas.

Police officers volunteer to paint faces at a this Children's Day celebration.

Teachers' Day is one week later, on September 17. It honors a priest named José Trinidad Reyes. He helped start the first Honduran university in the 1800s. Schools close, and students make cards and give their teachers small gifts such as fruit.

Did You Know?
José Trinidad Reyes's birthday was on June 11. It is now celebrated as Students' Day. High school students get this day off school.

Teachers' Day shows how important teachers are to students and the country.

Independence Day

Spain ruled Honduras until September 15, 1812. On that day, Honduras became free from Spanish control. Hondurans celebrate their Independence Day every year. Schools and businesses across the country close for the holiday.

Did You Know?
Hondurans celebrate their Flag Day on September 1. It begins events across the country that lead up to Independence Day.

Soldiers, such as these on horseback, show off their skills during parades.

Hondurans' love of their country is easy to see on Independence Day. People get up early for a long day of parades. Parades include dancers, cheerleaders, and marching bands. Everyone wears bright costumes. The parades are big, and can last for hours! Later, families and friends hold fiestas.

Schools, marching bands, and the military all take part in Independence Day parades. These Navy cadets are showing off their marching skills in a parade.

Honduras joined with other parts of Central America after it was free of Spain's control. Honduran Francisco Morazán was president of the **Federal Republic of Central America** (1830–38). This federation later fell apart due to disagreements between the countries. Morazán's enemies killed him. Today he is remembered for trying to keep Central America together.

A large parade of Honduran soldiers takes place in Tegucigalpa on Francisco Morazán Day.

Each year, Honduras honors Morazán on his birthday, October 3. Francisco Morazán Day is also called Soldiers Day. The government chose this day to remember its soldiers because Francisco Morazán was a soldier. Schools also put on parades. They praise Morazán's fight to bring together Central America.

Did You Know?
Honduras also honors its armed forces on October 21 each year. This holiday is called Army Day.

Francisco Morazán is shown on statues throughout the country, such as this one in Tegucigalpa. He also appears on the 5 lempira bill.

Día de la Raza

Día de la Raza started out as Columbus Day. It remembers Christopher Columbus landing in the **New World** on October 12, 1492. In Honduras, this day no longer honors Columbus's arrival and Spanish rule. Instead, on October 12, Hondurans honor the unity of the cultures in the country.

Did You Know?
Christopher Columbus is not popular in Honduras. He and other Europeans did great harm to Indigenous peoples there.

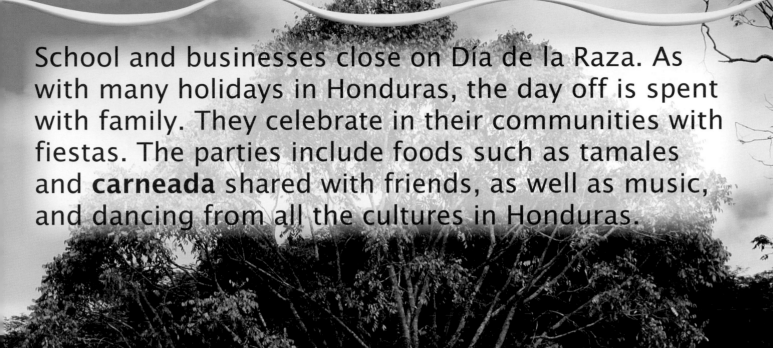

School and businesses close on Día de la Raza. As with many holidays in Honduras, the day off is spent with family. They celebrate in their communities with fiestas. The parties include foods such as tamales and **carneada** shared with friends, as well as music, and dancing from all the cultures in Honduras.

Did You Know?
Día de la Raza now celebrates all of the cultures of Honduras, including Indigenous peoples. These children are studying the culture of the ancient Maya and mural making.

Christmas Time

Some Hondurans begin the Christmas season with Posada. For nine nights, they re-enact the Bible story of Mary and Joseph looking for a place to stay. They carry homemade **nativity scenes** to three neighbors. It ends on Christmas Eve, which is called Noche Buena. It means "Good Night" in Spanish.

Santa Claus and elves visit Honduran children in their neighborhood.

On December 24, many Hondurans get a new outfit and shoes. Families enjoy their big holiday dinner late that night. It often includes foods such as tamales and roasted pork. At midnight, many places have fireworks. Fiestas carry on until early morning. December 25 is a quiet day spent visiting with family. They eat leftovers from the feast.

Tamales are a mix of meat and vegetables with rice or corn folded in a banana leaf, then steamed.

A nativity scene is decorated with lights in Tegucigalpa.

Glossary

carneada A Honduran beef dish flavored with orange and cumin and cooked on a barbeque

Central America An area of land south of Mexico that includes Guatemala, Belize, El Salvador, Honduras, Nicaragua, Costa Rica, and Panama

ethnic Sharing a common culture, religion, or language

exiled Expelled or sent sent someone away from their native land

Federal Republic of Central America A state (1821–1841) made up of several of Spain's former Central American territories. The territories are now the countries of Honduras, Guatemala, El Salvador, Nicaragua, and Costa Rica.

Indigenous Living, growing, or occurring naturally in a particular place

Lenca An Indigenous people of Honduras

nativity scene A scene showing the Baby Jesus with his mother Mary, father Joseph, and Three Kings

New World The term used to describe Earth's western hemisphere

Organization of American States A group of North American countries banded together for economic, cultural, and military cooperation

patron saint A holy person who is believed to protect a certain place or certain people

piñata A paper mache figure filled with candies or toys that is traditionally cracked open during a game at birthdays

re-enact To act out an event that happened in the past

Roman Catholic A Christian church centered in Rome, Italy, with the Pope as its leader

settler A person who comes to live in a new territory or country

Virgin Mary The mother of Jesus Christ, the son of God, in the Christian religion

Index